90 Day

SARAH'S SECRET
PLAY MORE-WORRY LESS

Sarah's
SECRET
Message is on the Last Page!
Shhh... Keep it a secret.

Name:

Date:

Email:

Phone#:

Address:

HOW TO GET OUT OF SURVIVAL MODE:

You can't do it all,
but you can do a lot.

You have big dreams,
and your life is so demanding.

Maybe you wonder how
you will ever
accomplish anything important.

HERE'S THE PLAN:

Do FOUR important things
every day for 90 days.
If you skip a day, just begin again!

If you write down your four goals every morning,
or every night before you go to bed, you might
actually change your life, live your dreams,
and get out of survival mode.

Start Today.
Turn the Page!

DAY 1

Date: 1-3-22

Choose **FOUR** <u>important</u> things
that you can accomplish today.

Ride my 300th Ride

Pack some Clothes

Reflect on Yesterday's Accomplishments:

DAY 2

Date: 1-4-22

Choose **FOUR** <u>necessary</u> things that you can accomplish today.

Get kids school work completed

finish Laundry and Packing

My Dreams for Tomorrow:

DAY 3

Date:_____

Choose **FOUR** <u>important</u> things
that you can accomplish today.

Reflect on Yesterday's Accomplishments:

DAY 4

Date:_____

Choose **FOUR** <u>necessary</u> things
that you can accomplish today.

My Dreams for Tomorrow:

_____
_____
_____

DAY 5

Date:_____
Choose **FOUR** <u>important</u> things
that you can accomplish today.

Reflect on Yesterday's Accomplishments:

DAY 6

Date:_____

Choose **FOUR** <u>necessary</u> things
that you can accomplish today.

My Dreams for Tomorrow:

_____
_____
_____

DAY 7

Date:_____

Choose **FOUR** <u>important</u> things
that you can accomplish today.

Reflect on Yesterday's Accomplishments:

_____
_____
_____

DAY 8

Date:_____

Choose **FOUR** <u>necessary</u> things that you can accomplish today.

My Dreams for Tomorrow:

_____
_____
_____

DAY 9

Date:_____

Choose **FOUR** <u>important</u> things
that you can accomplish today.

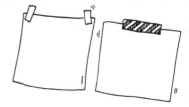

Reflect on Yesterday's Accomplishments:

_____
_____
_____

DAY 10

Date:_____

Choose **FOUR** <u>necessary</u> things that you can accomplish today.

My Dreams for Tomorrow:

_____

_____

_____

DAY 11

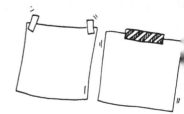

Date:_____

Choose **FOUR** <u>important</u> things
that you can accomplish today.

Reflect on Yesterday's Accomplishments:

_____

_____

_____

DAY 12

Date:_____

Choose **FOUR** <u>necessary</u> things that you can accomplish today.

My Dreams for Tomorrow:

_____

_____

_____

DAY 13

Date:_____

Choose **FOUR** <u>important</u> things
that you can accomplish today.

Reflect on Yesterday's Accomplishments:

DAY 14

Date:_____

Choose **FOUR** <u>necessary</u> things that you can accomplish today.

My Dreams for Tomorrow:

DAY 15

Date:_____

Choose **FOUR** <u>important</u> things
that you can accomplish today.

Reflect on Yesterday's Accomplishments:

DAY 16

Date:_____

Choose **FOUR** <u>necessary</u> things that you can accomplish today.

My Dreams for Tomorrow:

_____
_____
_____

DAY 17

Date:_____

Choose **FOUR** <u>important</u> things
that you can accomplish today.

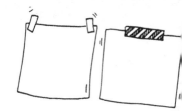

Reflect on Yesterday's Accomplishments:

DAY 18

Date:_____

Choose **FOUR** <u>necessary</u> things that you can accomplish today.

My Dreams for Tomorrow:

_____

_____

_____

DAY 19

Date:_____

Choose **FOUR** <u>important</u> things
that you can accomplish today.

Reflect on Yesterday's Accomplishments:

DAY 20

Date:_____

Choose **FOUR** <u>necessary</u> things that you can accomplish today.

My Dreams for Tomorrow:

_____
_____
_____
_____

DAY 21

Date:_____

Choose **FOUR** <u>important</u> things
that you can accomplish today.

Reflect on Yesterday's Accomplishments:

_____
_____
_____

DAY 22

Date:_____

Choose **FOUR** <u>necessary</u> things
that you can accomplish today.

My Dreams for Tomorrow:

_____
_____
_____

DAY 23

Date:_____

Choose **FOUR** <u>important</u> things
that you can accomplish today.

Reflect on Yesterday's Accomplishments:

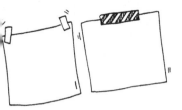

DAY 24

Date:_____

Choose **FOUR** <u>necessary</u> things that you can accomplish today.

My Dreams for Tomorrow:

_____
_____
_____

DAY 25

Date:_____

Choose **FOUR** <u>important</u> things
that you can accomplish today.

Reflect on Yesterday's Accomplishments:

_____
_____
_____

DAY 26

Date:_____

Choose **FOUR** <u>necessary</u> things
that you can accomplish today.

My Dreams for Tomorrow:

_____
_____
_____

DAY 27

Date:_____

Choose **FOUR** <u>important</u> things
that you can accomplish today.

Reflect on Yesterday's Accomplishments:

DAY 28

Date:_____

Choose **FOUR** <u>necessary</u> things that you can accomplish today.

My Dreams for Tomorrow:

_____
_____
_____
_____

DAY 29

Date:_____

Choose **FOUR** <u>important</u> things
that you can accomplish today.

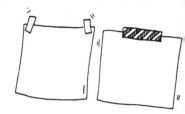

Reflect on Yesterday's Accomplishments:

DAY 30

Date:_____

Choose **FOUR** <u>necessary</u> things
that you can accomplish today.

My Dreams for Tomorrow:

_____
_____
_____

DAY 31

Date:_____

Choose **FOUR** <u>important</u> things
that you can accomplish today.

Reflect on Yesterday's Accomplishments:

_____
_____
_____

DAY 32

Date:_____

Choose **FOUR** <u>necessary</u> things that you can accomplish today.

My Dreams for Tomorrow:

_____
_____
_____

DAY 33

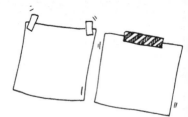

Date:_____

Choose **FOUR** <u>important</u> things
that you can accomplish today.

Reflect on Yesterday's Accomplishments:

_____
_____
_____

DAY 34

Date:_____

Choose **FOUR** <u>necessary</u> things
that you can accomplish today.

My Dreams for Tomorrow:

_____
_____
_____

DAY 35

Date:_____

Choose **FOUR** <u>important</u> things
that you can accomplish today.

Reflect on Yesterday's Accomplishments:

DAY 36

Date:_____

Choose **FOUR** <u>necessary</u> things
that you can accomplish today.

My Dreams for Tomorrow:

_____
_____
_____

DAY 37

Date:_____

Choose **FOUR** <u>important</u> things
that you can accomplish today.

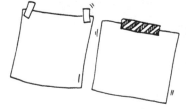

Reflect on Yesterday's Accomplishments:

_____
_____
_____

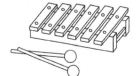

Date:_____

Choose **FOUR** <u>necessary</u> things
that you can accomplish today.

My Dreams for Tomorrow:

_____
_____
_____

DAY 39

Date:_____

Choose **FOUR** <u>important</u> things
that you can accomplish today.

Reflect on Yesterday's Accomplishments:

_____
_____
_____

DAY 40

Date:_____

Choose **FOUR** <u>necessary</u> things
that you can accomplish today.

My Dreams for Tomorrow:

_____

_____

_____

DAY 41

Date:_____

Choose **FOUR** <u>important</u> things
that you can accomplish today.

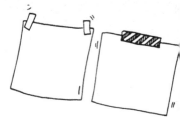

Reflect on Yesterday's Accomplishments:

DAY 42

Date:_____

Choose **FOUR** <u>necessary</u> things
that you can accomplish today.

My Dreams for Tomorrow:

_____

_____

_____

DAY 43

Date:_____

Choose **FOUR** <u>important</u> things
that you can accomplish today.

Reflect on Yesterday's Accomplishments:

DAY 44

Date:_____

Choose **FOUR** <u>necessary</u> things that you can accomplish today.

My Dreams for Tomorrow:

_____
_____
_____

DAY 45

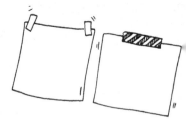

Date:_____

Choose **FOUR** <u>important</u> things
that you can accomplish today.

Reflect on Yesterday's Accomplishments:

_____
_____
_____

DAY 46

Date:_____

Choose **FOUR** <u>necessary</u> things that you can accomplish today.

My Dreams for Tomorrow:

_____

_____

_____

DAY 47

Date:_____

Choose **FOUR** <u>important</u> things
that you can accomplish today.

Reflect on Yesterday's Accomplishments:

DAY 48

Date:_____

Choose **FOUR** <u>necessary</u> things that you can accomplish today.

My Dreams for Tomorrow:

_____

_____

_____

DAY 49

Date:_____

Choose **FOUR** <u>important</u> things
that you can accomplish today.

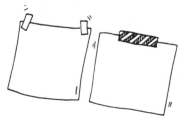

Reflect on Yesterday's Accomplishments:

Date:_____

Choose **FOUR** <u>necessary</u> things
that you can accomplish today.

My Dreams for Tomorrow:

_____
_____
_____

DAY 51

Date:_____

Choose **FOUR** <u>important</u> things
that you can accomplish today.

Reflect on Yesterday's Accomplishments:

_____
_____
_____

DAY 52

Date:_____

Choose **FOUR** <u>necessary</u> things
that you can accomplish today.

My Dreams for Tomorrow:

_____
_____
_____
_____

DAY 53

Date:_____

Choose **FOUR** <u>important</u> things
that you can accomplish today.

Reflect on Yesterday's Accomplishments:

_____

_____

_____

DAY 54

Date:_____

Choose **FOUR** <u>necessary</u> things that you can accomplish today.

My Dreams for Tomorrow:

_____

_____

_____

DAY 55

Date:_____

Choose **FOUR** <u>important</u> things
that you can accomplish today.

Reflect on Yesterday's Accomplishments:

DAY 56

Date:_____

Choose **FOUR** <u>necessary</u> things
that you can accomplish today.

My Dreams for Tomorrow:

DAY 57

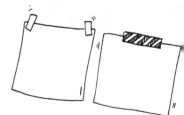

Date:_____

Choose **FOUR** <u>important</u> things
that you can accomplish today.

Reflect on Yesterday's Accomplishments:

_____
_____
_____

DAY 58

Date:_____

Choose **FOUR** <u>necessary</u> things
that you can accomplish today.

My Dreams for Tomorrow:

_____

_____

_____

DAY 59

Date:_____

Choose **FOUR** <u>important</u> things
that you can accomplish today.

Reflect on Yesterday's Accomplishments:

DAY 60

Date:_____

Choose **FOUR** <u>necessary</u> things
that you can accomplish today.

My Dreams for Tomorrow:
_____
_____
_____

DAY 61

Date:_____

Choose **FOUR** <u>important</u> things
that you can accomplish today.

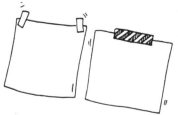

Reflect on Yesterday's Accomplishments:

DAY 62

Date:_____

Choose **FOUR** <u>necessary</u> things that you can accomplish today.

My Dreams for Tomorrow:

DAY 63

Date:_____

Choose **FOUR** <u>important</u> things
that you can accomplish today.

Reflect on Yesterday's Accomplishments:

DAY 64

Choose **FOUR** <u>necessary</u> things
that you can accomplish today.

My Dreams for Tomorrow:

_____
_____
_____

DAY 65

Date:_____

Choose **FOUR** <u>important</u> things
that you can accomplish today.

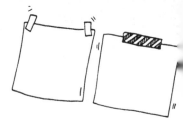

Reflect on Yesterday's Accomplishments:

DAY 66

Date:_____

Choose **FOUR** <u>necessary</u> things that you can accomplish today.

My Dreams for Tomorrow:

_____
_____
_____

DAY 67

Date:_____

Choose **FOUR** <u>important</u> things
that you can accomplish today.

Reflect on Yesterday's Accomplishments:

_____
_____
_____

DAY 68

Date:_____

Choose **FOUR** <u>necessary</u> things that you can accomplish today.

My Dreams for Tomorrow:
_____
_____
_____

DAY 69

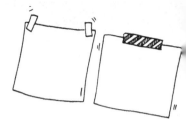

Date:_____

Choose **FOUR** <u>important</u> things that you can accomplish today.

Reflect on Yesterday's Accomplishments:

DAY 70

Date:_____

Choose **FOUR** <u>necessary</u> things that you can accomplish today.

My Dreams for Tomorrow:

_____
_____
_____

DAY 71

Date:_____

Choose **FOUR** <u>important</u> things
that you can accomplish today.

Reflect on Yesterday's Accomplishments:

DAY 72

Date:_____

Choose **FOUR** <u>necessary</u> things
that you can accomplish today.

My Dreams for Tomorrow:

DAY 73

Date:_____

Choose **FOUR** <u>important</u> things
that you can accomplish today.

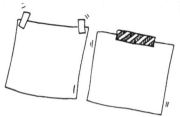

Reflect on Yesterday's Accomplishments:

DAY 74

Date:_____

Choose **FOUR** <u>necessary</u> things that you can accomplish today.

My Dreams for Tomorrow:

_____
_____
_____

DAY 75

Date:_____

Choose **FOUR** <u>important</u> things
that you can accomplish today.

Reflect on Yesterday's Accomplishments:

DAY 76

Choose **FOUR** <u>necessary</u> things
that you can accomplish today.

My Dreams for Tomorrow:

_____

_____

_____

DAY 77

Date:_____

Choose **FOUR** <u>important</u> things
that you can accomplish today.

Reflect on Yesterday's Accomplishments:

_____
_____
_____

Date:_____

Choose **FOUR** <u>necessary</u> things that you can accomplish today.

My Dreams for Tomorrow:

_____
_____
_____

DAY 79

Date:_____

Choose **FOUR** <u>important</u> things
that you can accomplish today.

Reflect on Yesterday's Accomplishments:

_____
_____
_____

DAY 80

Date:_____

Choose **FOUR** <u>necessary</u> things
that you can accomplish today.

My Dreams for Tomorrow:

_____
_____
_____

DAY 81

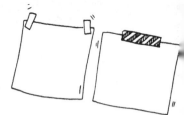

Date:_____

Choose **FOUR** <u>important</u> things
that you can accomplish today.

Reflect on Yesterday's Accomplishments:

DAY 82

Date:_____

Choose **FOUR** <u>necessary</u> things
that you can accomplish today.

My Dreams for Tomorrow:

_____
_____
_____

DAY 83

Date:_____

Choose **FOUR** <u>important</u> things
that you can accomplish today.

Reflect on Yesterday's Accomplishments:

DAY 84

Date:_____

Choose **FOUR** <u>necessary</u> things
that you can accomplish today.

My Dreams for Tomorrow:

_____
_____
_____

DAY 85

Date:_____

Choose **FOUR** <u>important</u> things
that you can accomplish today.

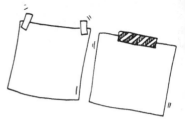

Reflect on Yesterday's Accomplishments:

_____
_____
_____

DAY 86

Date:_____

Choose **FOUR** <u>necessary</u> things that you can accomplish today.

My Dreams for Tomorrow:
_____
_____
_____

DAY 87

Date:_____

Choose **FOUR** <u>important</u> things
that you can accomplish today.

Reflect on Yesterday's Accomplishments:

DAY 88

Date:_____

Choose **FOUR** <u>necessary</u> things
that you can accomplish today.

My Dreams for Tomorrow:

_____
_____
_____

DAY 89

Date:_____

Choose **FOUR** <u>important</u> things
that you can accomplish today.

Reflect on Yesterday's Accomplishments:

DAY 90

Date:_____

Choose **FOUR** <u>necessary</u> things
that you can accomplish today.

My Dreams for Tomorrow:

_____

_____

_____

Just for Fun

My Notes:

My Notes:

Just for Fun

My Notes:

Just for Fun

My Notes:

Just for Fun

My Notes:

Just for Fun

My Notes:

Just for Fun

My Notes:

Just for Fun

My Notes:

My Notes:

Just for Fun

My Notes:

Just for Fun

My Notes:

SARAH'S SECRET MESSAGE

PLAY IS IMPORTANT!

Sometimes we feel like we don't have time to play. We often feel like the serious things in life matter more than the fun things in life. Sometimes we all need to stop doing "grown up things" to do the thing that bring joy into your life! Do the things that bring joy into the lives of the people around you.

HERE ARE SOME WAYS TO PLAY MORE:

Play an Instrument. Play a record. Play a board game. Play a sport. Play with a child. Play hide and seek. Play catch. Play your favorite song. Play with pet. Play your favorite musical, and watch it with a friend. Play house. Play with your sweetie. Smile more.

Be intentional about play, because play matters.

When you think of the four goals you have for each day, make sure at least one of them is playful.

Made in the USA
Las Vegas, NV
07 December 2021

36379636R00066